Mr. Kean's Garden

Ann Weil
Illustrated by Scott Goto

Rigby
A Harcourt Achieve Imprint

www.Rigby.com
1-800-531-5015

Level O Guided Reading Chapter Book

On Our Way to English: *Mr. Kean's Garden*

© 2004 by Rigby
1000 Hart Road
Barrington, IL 60010
www.rigby.com

Text by Ann Weil
Illustrated by Scott Goto

09 08 07
10 9 8 7 6 5 4 3 2 1A

Printed in China

ISBN 0-7578-4392-1

Contents

Chapter One
The Vegetable Garden 5

Chapter Two
An Accident in the Garden 11

Chapter Three
A Special Visit 18

Chapter Four
The Surprise 25

Chapter One

The Vegetable Garden

The rocks on the driveway made a crunching sound as Josela stopped her bike in front of her house.

"Hi, *Abuelita!*" she called to her grandmother. "I got home before Alberto today!"

"That's not fair!" shouted her older brother as he stopped next to her. "You left school ten minutes before I did."

"It was only five minutes!" yelled Josela.

"Enough arguing, you two," said Grandma. "Come in and have some corn bread while it's still hot."

Josela and Alberto jumped off their bikes and ran toward the house.

"Yum," said Alberto, "this is great corn bread, Grandma."

"Now," said Grandma, "before you eat it all, take some of it next door to Mr. Kean."

The children ran next door and knocked on the front door, but Mr. Kean wasn't there. They thought he might be in his garden.

Josela and Alberto found Mr. Kean pulling weeds in his garden. The children knew that Mr. Kean loved gardening and that his garden had won many awards.

"Thank you very much, children," Mr. Kean said as he took the corn bread from Josela. "Your grandmother is a wonderful cook." He stood up, cut some tulips from his garden, and handed them to Josela. "Please take these to her and tell her thank you."

"They're beautiful," Josela said as she carefully held the flowers.

"What are these?" asked Alberto as he pointed to some tiny green things poking out of the ground.

"Those are radishes," replied Mr. Kean, "and these are carrots. I also have corn, peas, beets, and beans."

"What about the plants in these little pots?" asked Josela.

"Those are tomato plants that I started growing indoors from seeds. Since it's time to plant them outside, maybe you could help me," said Mr. Kean.

Then they heard their grandfather calling their names from next door.

"It's dinner time," said Alberto as he looked at his watch.

"But I want to work in the garden," groaned Josela.

Mr. Kean suggested that they should come back on Saturday morning and help him plant the potatoes.

"Will they be easy to plant?" asked Josela.

"You'll find out on Saturday," Mr. Kean said as he waved goodbye. "Wear old clothes because gardening can get messy!"

Chapter 2

An Accident in the Garden

Josela woke up early on Saturday morning and put on her blue jeans and a sweatshirt. Alberto was eating his breakfast when his sister ran into the kitchen.

"Let's go!" said Josela as she headed for the door.

"Not so fast, young lady," said Grandpa. "Sit down and have some breakfast first because you will need your strength to work all morning in Mr. Kean's garden."

"Welcome back to my garden!" exclaimed Mr. Kean, who was already working in the garden.

"What are we going to do first?" asked Josela.

"We can start with the potatoes if you both help me dig the holes."

"Sure, but first, what's that round black thing on the side of the path?" Alberto asked.

"That is a worm farm," explained Mr. Kean. "I put pieces of food in one part of it, the worms eat their way through it, and they leave behind good plant food."

Alberto grabbed a fat worm and began to chase Josela with it. "Here's a surprise for you," he teased.

Josela screamed as Alberto wiggled the worm in front of her face.

"Are you all right, Josela?" called Mr. Kean.

Before Josela could answer, the children heard a crash and a yell. Mr. Kean had tripped over a rake as he was going to see why Josela was screaming.

"Mr. Kean, are you okay?" cried Josela as she rushed over to him.

He was sitting on the ground, rubbing his leg. "I don't think I can stand up," he said.

Alberto called for his grandfather to come and help.

"Can we come with you to the hospital?" asked Josela as her grandfather helped Mr. Kean into the taxi that had come to take him to the hospital.

"No, Josela, there's not enough room in the taxi for all of us," answered Grandpa as he sat down next to Mr. Kean.

Josela and Alberto waved sadly as the taxi drove away.

"What's that on the ground?" asked Alberto as he pointed to an envelope on the sidewalk in front of them.

Josela saw Mr. Kean's name on the envelope. "I think that it fell out of Mr. Kean's pocket," she answered as she bent down to pick it up.

The envelope already had a stamp on it, so Josela ran to the corner and put it in the mailbox.

Chapter 3

A Special Visit

"When will Mr. Kean be able to come home?" Josela asked at dinner that night.

"I'm not sure," said Grandpa, "but it will be at least a couple of days. Luckily, Mr. Kean's break wasn't that bad, but he won't be able to walk for at least a month."

"He asked me to bring you both to visit him tomorrow," added Grandma. "He has something very important to ask."

The next morning, Josela, Alberto, and Grandma took the bus to the hospital. Josela was carrying a box of cookies that Grandma had baked for Mr. Kean.

"This place is so big," said Josela as they entered the four-story building. (Josela and Alberto had never been inside of a hospital before.) "How will we ever find Mr. Kean?"

"Mr. Kean is meeting us in the hospital garden," Grandma said as they walked through a door and into a small outdoor garden.

Mr. Kean was already there, sitting in a wheelchair with his broken leg in a cast.

"We brought you these cookies," Josela said as cheerfully as she could. (After all, Mr. Kean wouldn't be here if it hadn't been for her and Alberto.)

"Thank you," said Mr. Kean as he opened the box and ate a cookie. "These are delicious. Would you like one?" Josela and Alberto each took a cookie.

"Grandma said that you had something important to ask us, Mr. Kean," Alberto said.

"Yes, I would like for you to plant my potatoes since I won't be able to do it myself."

Josela was glad to be able to help Mr. Kean, so she said, "Sure, but how do we do it?"

21

"Potatoes grow better if there are ashes in the dirt around them, so you will need to collect the ashes from the fireplace in my living room," Mr. Kean explained. "Then mix the ashes with the dirt around the potatoes when you plant them." He handed Grandma the key to his back door.

"The potatoes are in the shed, and the key is under the watering can," Mr. Kean added.

"Should we feed your cat for you while we are at your house?" asked Josela.

"No, my neighbor Mrs. Kovalov said that she would do that for me," said Mr. Kean.

Mr. Kean looked tired, so Grandma and the children said goodbye.

"Let's get the ashes right now," Alberto said when they got home.

He and Josela ran to Mr. Kean's house and used the key to get in the back door. Finding plenty of ashes in the fireplace, Alberto scooped them all into a bucket.

Suddenly they heard a key turning in the front door. Josela and Alberto glanced at each other and then looked at the door. They knew that Mr. Kean wouldn't be coming home yet, so who could it be?

Chapter 4

The Surprise

It was Mrs. Kovalov! "What are you two doing in here?" she cried. "You scared me!"

Josela felt the same way. "We're getting ashes from the fireplace to plant with Mr. Kean's potatoes."

Mrs. Kovalov thought it was nice that they wanted to help while Mr. Kean was in the hospital. As Josela and Alberto walked outside to the shed, they heard Mrs. Kovalov pouring cat food into the cat's dish.

Alberto found the key under the watering can and opened the door to the shed.

"Look, here is a book about growing vegetables," said Josela. "There's a chapter on potatoes, and it says that potatoes need ashes. Mr. Kean sure knows a lot about gardening!"

The children mixed the ashes with the dirt and carefully planted the potatoes.

"We still have an hour until dinner time," said Alberto as he checked his watch.

"I saw some seeds in the shed, so I guess we could plant those for Mr. Kean, too," said Josela. "The gardening book will probably tell us how to do it."

One week later, Mr. Kean came home from the hospital, but he had to stay in his wheelchair and couldn't get to the garden. So Mr. Kean didn't know that Josela and Alberto were using his gardening book to care for his garden.

A few weeks later, two people knocked on Mr. Kean's front door. (They were the two garden judges who had given Mr. Kean first prize for his garden last year.)

Mr. Kean was surprised to see them because he didn't remember sending in the entry form for the gardening contest this year. "I'm so sorry you made the trip for nothing," he told them.

One of the judges said, "We just met your two young helpers outside, and your garden looks even better than it did last year, Mr. Kean. It looks as if they have worked very hard."

After the judges left, Josela and Alberto came inside. Mr. Kean could see that their hands were very dirty.

"What have you two been up to?" Mr. Kean asked in a serious voice, but with a smile on his face.

They told him about finding and mailing his envelope for the contest. Then they explained that they had used the gardening book in the shed, and had planted all of the seeds.

"It was a lot of fun," said Josela.

"It was also a lot of work!" added Alberto.

With the cast finally off of his leg, Mr. Kean was able to go out into his garden. "You children are wonderful," he said as he looked around at the many kinds of plants.

"The gardening book says that the potatoes can be dug up now," Josela said. Alberto carefully dug up the first plant, and Josela lifted out the potatoes.

"This is so much fun!" she said.

"Good morning," called Mrs. Kovalov from the gate. "I was just bringing you a cake. Are all of these beautiful vegetables from your garden, Mr. Kean?" she asked.

"Yes, and these two children are super gardeners!" replied Mr. Kean.

"I have so many weeds in my garden," said Mrs. Kovalov. "Will you help me, too?"

"As long as you promise not to break your leg!" laughed Alberto.